ALIBI

Elsa Morante

ALIBI

&
Appendix

NARCISSUS

Translated from the Italian by

Anthony Barnett

Paintings, Drawings by

Monica Ferrando

A·B

Elsa Morante
Alibi

Longanesi, Milan, 1958
Garzanti, Milan, 1988
with Appendix Narciso
Einaudi, Torino, 2004, 2012

Italian original
Copyright © Einaudi & TILA
for The Estate of Elsa Morante 2004
Translation Copyright © Anthony Barnett 2024
Paintings, Drawings Copyright © Monica Ferrando 2024

Anthony Barnett is hereby identified as the moral rights
holder of the translation in this version of the work and
Monica Ferrando of the paintings, drawings in this work

All rights reserved
reprinting or online posting in whole or in
part without the written permission of the
copyright holders is prohibited except
for short quotation as allowed in
fair use in such as a review

Typeset in Centaur MT by AB©omposer

Printed by TJ Books Padstow

Published 2024 by
Allardyce Book ABP
14 Mount Street · Lewes · East Sussex BN7 1HL [E]UK
www.abar.net

Distributed in USA by SPD
www.spdbooks.org

CIP records for this book are available from
The British Library and The Library of Congress

ISBN 978-0-907954-71-2

Translator's Note

I am indebted to Giorgio Agamben's essay "Taking Leave of Tragedy" in *The End of the Poem*, Stanford, 1999, for learning about Elsa Morante's poetry, which often interweaves myths and fables with private affairs laid bare, almost, and includes tributes to her beloved cats. Stanza breaks here follow the text established in the 2004 edition, in which *Narciso* first appears as a posthumous appendix, with an introduction by Cesare Garboli. Morante's often idiosyncratic* syntax and punctuation, or sometimes lack thereof, are closely followed, as is her capitalization, with a few exceptions. If we should believe Morante's making light of her poems in her preamble, or short preface, it becomes clear that Agamben holds them in higher regard than does the Author herself. My thanks to Timothy Harris, whose work in Tokyo, where he lives, has included writing, translation, theatre, for many fruitful discussions, and who really should be considered the co-translator of "Hamlet", but, of course, I alone am responsible for any remaining infelicities. And my heartfelt thanks to Monica Ferrando for her paintings, drawings and advice.

*I was going to add "though reasoned" only I am minded of Alan Garner's introduction to his *Collected Folk Tales*: "When literary styles, based on reason, try to make sense of folk tale, they render it mundane. The real meaning is in the music; it is in the language: not phonetics, grammar or syntax, but pitch and cadence, and the colour of the word."

—AB, January 2024

Monice Ferrando
Paintings, Drawings
January 2024

front cover oil on canvas, 100 x 70 cm
frontispiece pencil on paper, 19.5 x 15.5 cm
27 pencil on paper, 19.5 x 15.5 cm
31 sumi ink on rice paper, 25 x 21.5 cm
39 pencil on paper, 17.5 x 15.5 cm
44 sumi ink on rice paper, 25 x 20 cm
endpaper sumi ink on rice paper, 20 x 26 cm
back cover oil on canvas, 100 x 70 cm

Translator's Note 7

Preamble [Premessa] 9

Minna the Siamese [Minna la Siamese] 10
Poem for Saruzza [Poesia per Saruzza] 12
Amulet [Amuleto] 14
To a Young 'Un [A una bambina] 15
Sheherazade [Sheherazade] 16
Letter [Lettera] 17
For Fable [Alla favola] 19
To Personae [Ai personaggi] 20
Song for Alvaro the Cat [Canto per il gatto Alvaro] 21
Adventure [Avventura] 23
Alibi [Alibi] 28
On Nerina [Su Nerina] 33
Arturo's Island [L'isola di Arturo] 34
Allegory [Allegoria] 35
Hamlet [Amleto] 37
The Cat to the Birdie [Il gatto all'uccellino] 38

Narcissus [Narciso] 40

Entomological & Botanical Note 45

Preamble

The Author entreats readers to forgive her the small value and weight of these pages. For being, by her habit (as well as by her nature and destiny) a writer of stories in prose, her scarce verses are, in part, no more than an echo, or, if you like, a chorus, of her novels; and, in part, no more than an enjoyment, or play, in which she sometimes loves to indulge, without too much commitment, for the simple pleasure of music. If, then, she has persuaded herself to publish these verses (some of which, as can be seen from the dates at the end of each, go back to the early days of her youth), the Author has done so only in the hope of rendering to those who will read them a little of that rest, and enjoyment, that she herself derived from composing them.

Elsa Morante

Rome, March 1958

Minna the Siamese

I have a pet, a cat: her name is Minna.

What I put on her plate, she eats,
and what I put in her bowl, she drinks.

She jumps onto my lap, looks at me, then sleeps,
so that I forget she's there. But if then,
mindful, I call her name, an ear twitches
in her sleep: her sleep is shadowed by her name.

Joy to say, and thanks, she has a guitalele:
if I scratch her head, or her neck, sweet sounds.

When I think how many centuries and things separate the two of us,
I'm afraid. I'm afraid for myself: she knows nothing of that.
But if I see her playing with a thread, if I watch
her celestial irises, I'm cheerful again.

On celebratory feast days, which all the people celebrate,
I feel sorry for her, who does not mark the days.
So she can also celebrate, I give her a little fish for lunch;
why she doesn't understand: though she blissfully eats it up.

Heaven, for love of her, gave her claws, and teeth:
but, so gentle, she uses them just for fun.
I feel sorrow when I think that if I were to kill her
prosecution would not befall me, nor hell, nor prison.

She kisses me so much, sometimes I deceive myself I am dear to her,
but I know, another mistress, or me, it's all the same.
She follows me, so that I delude myself and think I must be everything,
but I know that my death would not touch her . . .

(1941)

Poem for Saruzza

Nine years since I said goodbye to you
O my forgotten, my young Sicilian.

Between the two of us lay
an inaccessible ruin
of distance and time,
and the bugler for the dead
on the passes sounds the silence.

But the echo of your laughter,
the last celestial farewell
wandered for nine years
across that desolate country
rebounding on the run, ephemeral
little girl. And your landfall
was what? Alone
I was in my room
today, and I was seized with amazement.
Suddenly I heard the echo
of your extinguished laughter.
I recognized you, and the pleasure
of a heartbeat coursed through me.

Thank you, fragile echo!
Beautiful canary flying
to this nest.
Sweet little fist poking
among these leaves.
A jewel of an orange aflame
on the calcinated wall.

Then, once again silence
in my memory,
and me in the empty room
a woman.

(Already a fever, there,
where my ear kisses me.)

(1943)

Amulet

When you pass by, and you call me,
I am absent.
Many long hours I have waited for you,
and you, distracted, fly off elsewhere.
No matter, the seraphic go-between
of our love,
the sultan of the zenith
who moves the spheres on the dial
with idle and holy fingers,
has already marked the moment
of our meeting.
Quietly my days turn
toward that imperious season.
She shines snow-white and glacial
rising upward, like a fire.
Ah, our enchanting room!
What do I care, treacherous spirit,
for your contrary thoughts?
The omen already bows its brow
at the announcement. Love and fate
unite you with me.

(1945)

To a Young 'Un

Your head of hair resembles the lustrous plumage
of a young black duck. Your eyes
are like mottled leaves. Your cheeks
are flecked with gold: and your pallor
loves the shade. Your perforated lobes
(as if stung by a bee)
are as red as the poppy
and naked. Such conceited piercing!
You do not have pendants like the others
nor a cross: and no godmother
to adorn you at the baptismal font.
Your mother in her conceit took care
to pierce your ears, but cared nothing
for your fate. They all say:
"Without gold a woman cannot marry",
and: "Born unbaptised, it's worse than being buried."
But you are on your own, curiosity
isn't for you.
I find a pretext and ask: "What are you called?"
You don't answer. "Don't you know
how to speak? Are you dumb?"
                                      Now
you look at me, distrustful,
and then you go back to your sullen games, beside
the iridescent pool.

(1945)

Scheherazade

My celestial bridegroom
(master of my breaths)
delays for me, benign,
my mortal sentence:
because among so many brides
I alone, only I,
know with wondrous tales
how to console the night.

It is not my virtue, but heaven's
has made me fantastical
if I am worthy of that grace.

And you, do not bear me envy,
nor, in spite, abandon
these felicitous vigils
for your inanimate sleeps.

For your delight, for my hope
summon the Dark.

(1946)

Letter

Everything that belongs to you, or emanates from you,
is rich with fabulous grace:
even your lovers, even my tears.
My envy covers with extraordinary charms
my rivals: they go by ways denied to mortals,
they have wise hearts, courtesy of angels.
And the tears you make me weep are my beautiful diadem,
should my bitter season be adorned with your smile.

I am amazed when I remember that I had so many wishes
and so many vows I did not know which one to choose.
Now, if a star falls in mid August,
if in the sea's sunset a virescent ray flashes,
if at supper I taste the first fruits of the new season,
or I bow to the sanctus bell of Elevation,
I have but one vow: your name, your name,
O word that opens for me the gate to paradise.

In my conceited heart, since you are sovereign there,
the ancient laws of the world are all overthrown:
pride is pleased to humble itself for you,
vanity hides before your glory,
desire turns into timid modesty,
my defeat rejoices in your victory,
wealth is happy to make itself, for you, poor,
and trespass and forgiveness, anxiety and rest,
blossom into a single flower, a grand double rose.

But the celestial phrase, which my mind hears,
Once again, I don't know how to tell you, there's no note or word.
I'll tell you: you are all my good, at every hour
this grace of loving you is my sweet company.
Let my affection console you as it consoles me,
O you who are my only intimate!

(1946)

For Fable

With you, Fiction, I gird my loins,
frivolous garb.
I work you with those golden plumes
which enfold me before becoming fire
my magificent departed season
transformed into a fulgurant phoenix!

The needle is red-hot, the cloth is smoke.
Consumed among its golden circles
lies the vainglorious hand
even in the game of *loves me loves me not*
the celestial answer
I fabricate.

(1947)

To Personae

You, Dead, magnificent hosts, welcome me
inside your royal mansions,
gracefully leaf through for me
your illuminated volumes.

I know: me, stupid and barbarous woman,
to you I am nothing but subject and handmaiden.
Nevertheless the golden fillet of your
exploits, and arrogant loves,
adorns my servile brow,
O deceitful Sultans.

I am nothing but a pronubial bee
amongst you, extraordinary and occult flowers.
Yet on my ephemeral elytra
however faint, a trace remains
of your celestial pollen.
And your honey
is all mine!

(1947)

Song for Alvaro the Cat

Your nest is in my arms,
O lazy, O glowing genius, O glossy,
O my frivolous! Midday and darkness
are your mansions, and you transform
from dove into an owl, and from tombs
you fly to the regions of smoke.
When all light is extinguished, your pupils
turn black, O doubler
of my drowsiness, and shatter
the solemn truce, blazing ephemeral
a thousand torches, childish tigers
chase one another in sweet delirium.
Then the feeble lamps rest
those that in the morning are the boast
of my windowsill, the twinflower
pretty eyes.

              And I was your equal!
Your equal! You, remember,
arrogant melancholy? Of leaves
dark and shining, a garden
we lived in together, among the barbarous
people of Paradise. For me it was exile,
but your room is still there,
and across my terra firma fleetingly passes
a playful pilgrim. Why do you grant me
your favour, O savage?

While your peers, celestial animals
savour mad indolences, before dawn fêtes
of heartless wars and hunts, why
are you here with me? Perennial, you, free, ingenuous,
and I have three things in store:
prison shame and death.
Among moons and suns, among shining thorns, grasses and chimeras
immortal young beasts leap,
gallant brothers with beautiful names: Curlicue,
Atropos, Violet, Passion Flower, Paloma,
in the magnificent storm of the first day . . .
And you? For love of me?

Won't you answer me? The confidences you envy
you imprison, like the Damascene sword stories of gold
in zebra skin velvet. Secrets of bazaars
are not told to women. Close your eyes and sing to me
cajoling cajoling your purring breaths,
my bee, spin your honeys.
The shadowy memory recedes
with every question I want to rest.
The joy of having you as a friend
suffices my heart. And of my tales and carnage
with your kisses, with your sweet cries,
you console me,
O cat of mine!

(1947)

Adventure

Do you have a heart? Legend has it that you do not.
On seeing me, the me consumed with love of you,
they all say: "Ah, crazy, into the mouths of sorcerers, pink with fables,
soldier of desperate undertakings, sailor without sail or oars,
where do you venture? into what deserts of sand,
following Morgan, and will-o'-the-wisps, and mocking larvae
you will quench your thirst in solitary death!
Ah, who cast this net for you, poor little fish?"
That's what people say; but let them say it!
To him who speaks ill of you, my enemy I swear.
For you, my capricious saint, divine countenance,
without arms without compass I set off.
No respite for hope ever.
I was born to difficult loves.

Like a rose in a garden
in far away Africa or Asia,
like a flag raised
atop a pirate ship,
like a silver shield
hung in a barbarous temple,
your heart shines uneasily
your frivolous, indolent heart,
your heroic, feminine heart,
your royal, untouched heart,
the heart of my love.
I believe in your heart!

The terrestrial grottos are all a jewel.
Funereal springtime for my vainglorious festivities,
violet amethyst and moon agate
and diamonds like iridescent roses
and vitrious topaz, golden topaz.
Their crystals have halos and fiery tails,
a thousand comets and moons for my night.
Gulfs offer me shells, and oceanic games,
and the boreal sky, rests and meditations.
Orange groves waft sweetnesses, like love's saliva,
and Asia, graceful beasts, my attentive slaves.
Majesties of kings converse with me,
and at my command circuses and theatres light up.
But I set out to conquer a sour fruit.
Your heart: other fruit I will not bite.
I do not want terrestrial gifts, I deny myself my power.
My only valour is this enterprise!
I set off to conquer a bitter fruit.
Bitter things are the dearest.

The room I seek of the precious heart is, I know, secret.
The journey to the nest of this coquette-phoenix
long and uncertain.
I am inexperienced,
I have neither companion nor guide,
but I shall arrive at the happy bower
of my beau, my idol.
Farewell, then, family, friends, farewell!

First one must ford the stagnant lake
of fear,
and cross the Grand Prides,
that spectacular series of cliffs.
One must root out insidious envy
and put to flight the monsters of jealousy,
(ah St Michael and St George, give me your shield!)
in ocular nights, purple forests,
where I may meet centaurs and hippogriffs,
and drink the magic blood of narcissi.
Next rise the triple walls of Sodom
around a foreign field
with seven crenellated towers.
I shall enchant the guardians,
redeem the bought brides,
I shall wander for ages through courtyards and staircases,
among a people of echoes and delusions
to the cherished door, which bears the cruel inscription:
Back, O pilgrim. Not welcome.

Ah, were I a winged nightingale, were I a centaur,
ah, were I mermaid,
were I Medoro or Nisus,
who perhaps would be more of a friend to you
one of theirs would be my name, gracious heart!
But no, Lisa is my name, born at the bitter hour
of noon, under the sign of the Lion,
a day of Christian rejoicing.
I was a simple girl,
my godmother was a cat,
and I set out to conquer a sweet heart.
Now that I have presented myself, be gracious, my love.
What are you afraid of, O animal? Of being caught in a trap?
Ah, no, I am not the daughter of the bitter pampas.
Of being stabbed? I have neither knife, nor stinger.
Nor am I a coppa, to throw you in prison,
nor a fairy, to have you as my companion night and day,
in the guise of a raven, in a golden cage.

Ah, do not judge me by my deed a hero!
My mind weighs less than fire,
and more than a curl of your tawny shock.
For my sorrow, for your vanquished love,
I want to play with you just a little
like a leaf plays with the shadow and the sun,
or a poppet with her red-coat cat.

And then I shall bid you goodbye.

You'll say: Lisa! You'll implore: Lisa!
Ah, Lisa! Lisa! you'll call. But I shall
say goodbye.

(1948)

Alibi

Only those who love know. Miserable those who do not love!
Like unconsecrated looks the holy hosts,
common and barren for him the thousand lives.
Only for him who loves, the Different lights up its splendours
and for him the house of two mysteries opens:
sorrowful mystery and joyful mystery.
    I love you. Blessèd is the moment
    I fell in love with you.

What is your name? Like the firmament
it changes with the hour. Are you Juliet? or are you Theodora?
are you called Arthur? or is it Nisus? Your name
serves only for play, like a bauta mask.
I would like to call you: *Fidele*; but it doesn't sound like you.

Your grace transforms
into a boast the scandal that surrounds you.
You are the bee and you are the rose.
You are the fate that colours the wings
and curls of your hair.
Your reverence is graceful like the rainbow.

Your days are a shining meadow
where you encounter fraternal angels:
the saintly, adult Chiron,
innocent Silenus, children with the feet of goats,
and dolphin-maidens in steely armour.
In the evening, you return to your wretched tiny room
and gaze at your destiny plotted with figures,

your dark sleeping companion
with his tattooed hide.

You were the favourite page at the court of the Orient,
you were the twin star son of Leda,
you were the best looking sailor on the Phoenician ship,
you were Alexander the glorious in his royal tent.
You were the prisoner whom the screws were forced to serve.
You were the valiant companion, the grace of the camp,
over whom the enemy who closes his eyes
weeps like a mother.
You were the dogaressa unravelling her purple hair
in the sun, on the terrace, high up among domes and banners.
You were the prima ballerina of Swan Lake,
you were Briseis, rosy-cheeked captive.
You were the saint who sings, closeted in the choir,
with a sweet contralto voice.
You were the Chinese princess with the childlike foot:
the Son of Heaven saw you, and fell in love.

Like a diamond is your palace
with a treasure in every room
and all the windows sparkling.
Your abode is an enchanted hive:
distant narcissi send you their honeys.
For your feasts, from distant eras
lights arrive, as to the firmament.
But you go into exile, alone and discontented.
>My child has neither home
>nor country.

The beautiful weft, adored by my heart,
is for you a bitter fold.
And for your salvation the bride never arrives
queen of the labyrinth.
For the strange taste of good and evil
your mouth is too sullen.
You are the ultimate fable. O flower of the hyacinth
one hundred racemes for a single solitary flower!

The haloed crowd in your beautiful game of mirrors
to you is desert and imposture.
But where are you off to? what are you looking for? in vain, cat-girl,
you're waiting for the passage of Oedipus across your path.
O fabulous question, for your delirium
there is no human answer.
Rest a while close to those who love you
my angel.

When you are close to me, you appear no more than a child.
My folded arms are all that's needed to nest you
and a cot is all you need for sleep.
But when you are distant, to me you become immense.
Your form is huge like Asia, your breath
is huge like the tides.
You scatter my black futile days
like a dust devil of black sand.
I run shouting your different names
along the unhearing gulf of death.

Rest a while close to those who love you.

Let me look at you. You swagger through my room
like a gallant striding
over a devastation of hearts.
In the mirror you admire your long lashes
you laugh like a jockey flying to the finish.
O my belovèd son, nocturnal rose!
Miserable like a cat in Neapolitan alleys
like the beggar and the poor pickpocket,
in elegance you surpass dukes and sovereigns
you shine like a gem from a mine
you change your diadem every night
you dress in gold like the autumns.

The lunar cashier strolls by with her white Great Danes...

Sleep.
Night that restores us to childhood
and like a beast defends its darlings
from offences of the day, spreads over us
its historical canopy.
Your colours, O childish morning,
you brought with you.
In funereal habitation, you too I forget.

Your beating heart is all of time.
You are the black night.

Your maternal body is my rest.

(1955)

On Nerina

Childhood memories. Without parents or ancestors
no one to disprove the legend.

Discordant and deaf notes,
unconnected dots and lines of inanimate chance
signifying nothing, drawing superb figures
within his days, historiated like the zodiac.
Subterranean gold mines
and in the air
arches and columns of gold.
The dolls' showcases shining like altars.

Festive terrestrial metropolises, and you, Laude, Jerusalem
of Sunday mornings!
You, in your new robe,
the equal of the Queen of Sheba . . .

Too long the waiting for the day.
She let herself be tempted into sleep.

(1955)

Arturo's Island

That, which you thought a tiny point on earth,
was everything.

And never shall this one treasure be stolen
from your jealous sleeping eyes.
Your first love shall never be violated.

Virginal she immured herself in night
like a gypsy child in her black shawl.
Star suspended in eternal boreal
sky: no treachery can touch her.

Young friends, more beautiful than Alexander and Euryalus,
forever beautiful, defend my fledgling's sleep.
Terror's insignia shall never cross the threshold
of this celestial isle.
                        Nor shall you know the law
that I, like many, learn,
—and it has shattered my heart:

outside limbo there is no elysium.

(1956)

Allegory

(Two Fables for N. N.)

I ~ AIDA

Once there was a slave girl, the Ethiopian Aida.

Thick curls cover her black forehead,
the theatre raves
over her voice, white like the moon.

Up in the gods, there was a dark spectator,
a black boy from Africa, barely out of childhood,
who, at first sight of her, falls in love
with the sweet Moorish singer,
and a fatal passion already consumes him.

The last scene is over,
with a childish heart, as if to a sister
he runs after her from the gallery.
He finds her in her dressing-room, before her mirror
unfastening a barbarous necklace,
and, there, on a Hamite lip
dies the name: AIDA . . .

For, make-up removed, this first
and only love, appears to him
in her regal features,
far off, white like the moon . . .

11 ~ NISUS

Once there was a horse named Nisus.
Tawny and delicate in hue, angelic her beauty.
She belonged to the stables of a count,
a pompous and coarse silk-stocking. But her heart
belonged to the jockey, who shared with her
the glory of their wins: a youngster, too, like Nisus,
and his mop of hair, like hers, russet.
                                        And when, at the race,
people shouted their two names together,
it was as if an infant centaur flew across the field:
Nisus and the jockey!
                        Meanwhile, the count's
getting ready to collect the day's prize.
But these two, they don't look at the prize:
they leave that to the count.
Lovefest's
enough for them both . . .

(1957)

Hamlet

Ah, the apparition of a weary dream,
ultimate penalty for accidie!
from obscure depths the boat resurfaces,
over and over: *other voices, other rooms.*

If only this anguished mind could
like water touch the root, surface like the green
to the topmost point. Insipid sap
foolish stem! always reborn to be enamoured
(with a puerile defenceless sigh)
of bold knights at sport in the chase
for angelic beasts.

(1957)

The Cat to The Birdie

Scherzo – Dedicated to S. P.

Hallali! Hallali!
On the perilous wire you, full of grace
you're resting, and taking flight you steal from me:
from me tail chasing in inane circles,
me futile minotaur forbidden flight.

O you blissful and helpless who song me
me miserable hunter armed with terrestrial claws!
You know I torment myself with you, O fragile and saintly
my repast unconsumed.

O life of my flesh, winged blood,
gallant spouse of birds,
O tenor
narcissus
feudatory to the most exalted heights.
Hallali! Hallali!
               And you of the monster laugh.

And a little earth mouse was my prey.

(1957)

NARCISSUS

I

O Reflection, O cherished and treacherous lover!
In you I know the fraternal face
of my iridescent desire.
Of the light I see in you
my light is made rich
and like flame in multiple mirrors
my secluded soul
chases itself in countless games.
You are the apparitions,
the ambiguous people of the sky
and demons white in the face
like roses.
In my dreams your figure
is despotic: it is you
red days, purple nights,
your Mask reigns in theatres.
Nor do I like to converse
except with Echo: supplicant
she runs to me, as I pass by
without companions, and calls:
"Narcissus! Narcissus! Narcissus!"

(Rome, 28 August 1945)

II

Where are you? insubstantial friend, where are you?
You are in water and in glass, vacuous splendours.
If I want to lose you the glass shatters.
Cold, colourless, water
slips through my furious fingers.
Vanishes disfigured, reappears untouched
like flowers in the meadow, all equal one to the other.
Your name is Desire,
you are the fire of lights, and the novice.
If I look into a stranger's eyes, I see you there again,
O diminutive chimera! Narcissus is painted
on a thousand mirrors! Of the living
you are the most mysterious. You are the only face
I am not allowed to look at in the flesh,
only in reflection and shadow, just
like the Holy Face.

(29 August 1945)

III

When I wake up, in the mornings, I look in the mirror.
Fire leaps from the ashes:
and you flash, O radiant face,
from the dust of sleep.
Like an elder brother, just as childlike
and motherly at heart, I scrutinize you
for signs of the night: one more
to number among the secret sequence!
Nights, like ants, march
in thousands under the earth. Of their tiny black legs, each
leaves the minutest trace:
obscure figures of an insane cabal!

Memory
is a church of deception: the naves are smoke,
the altars false. On the last
rambles an infant idol: his round face
your first, your first friend! Today you are other than the one
my mother kissed. You
are transient. A senile larva
I sometimes meet in omens
and I am chilled by the resemblance!
But, like memory, the omen
is a fib. The past and tomorrow
are smoke, blue consorts
of sleepless nights. Old age
cannot touch the face of adoration.
First, the burial mirror shattered,
Narcissus will lie on the bare
dry sand, gold on gold,
like the glowing medusa and the oceanic flora
when the sea drains.

(4 September 1945)

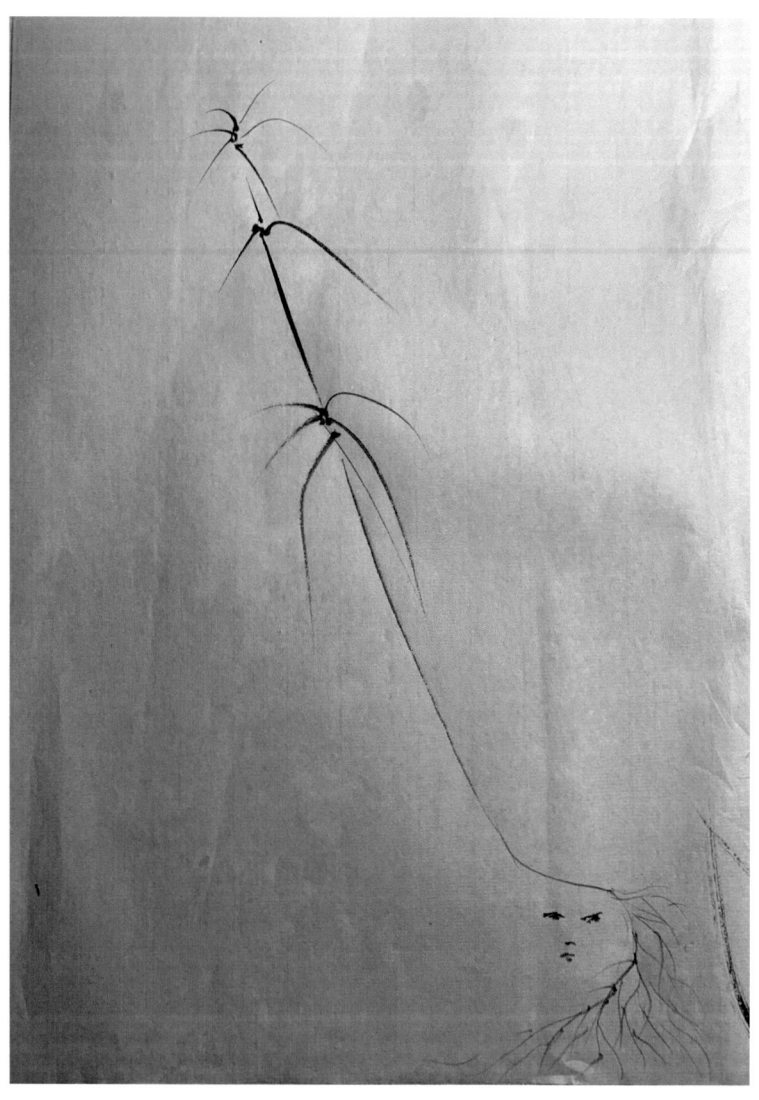

ENTOMOLOGICAL & BOTANICAL NOTE

In "Personnae" we note that "elytra", Italian "elitre", are the wing cases of beetles; bees do not have them, though we also note that for Morante hers are "effimere". In "Alibi" we note that hyacinths are not corymbose; they have "racemes", Italian "racemi", although Morante writes "cento corimbi". We believe Morante chooses "corimbi" because of its euphony, and also because of the word's secondary sense simply of "clusters", a sense that "corymb" does not have in English; so we prefer the botanically correct "racemes" for the translation.

ELSA MORANTE
(1912-1985)
novels include
Lies and Sorcery
Arturo's Island
History
other poetry
*The World Saved by Kids
and Other Epics*

MONICA FERRANDO
images and prose in English
with Giorgio Agamben
*The Unspeakable Girl:
The Myth and Mystery of Kore*
poems and images in *Snow lit rev* 11
https://www.monicaferrando.com

ANTHONY BARNETT
Italian interest
collected *Translations* incl. Zanzotto
Translations Addenda incl.
Pavese, Ungaretti, Zanzotto, and
essay on Leopardi's "The Infinite"
Antonyms Anew: Barbs & Loves incl.
essays on Saba, Zanzotto